**RECORDED VERSIONS GUITAR**

AUTHENTIC TRANSCRIPTIONS
WITH NOTES AND TABLATURE

*Sarah McLachlan* *Surfacing*

## CONTENTS

**Music transcriptions by** *Pete Billmann*

Front Cover and *Last Dance* Photos by *Dennis Keeley*; Title page photo by *Mark Van S*;
Design and Illustrations by *John Rummen*

ISBN 0-634-00496-4

**HAL•LEONARD®**
CORPORATION
7777 W. BLUEMOUND RD. P.O. BOX 13819 MILWAUKEE, WI 53213

Visit Hal Leonard Online at
**www.halleonard.com**

# Building a Mystery

**Words and Music by Sarah McLachlan and Pierre Marchand**

**Pre-Chorus**

7

**Chorus**

11

## Outro-Chorus

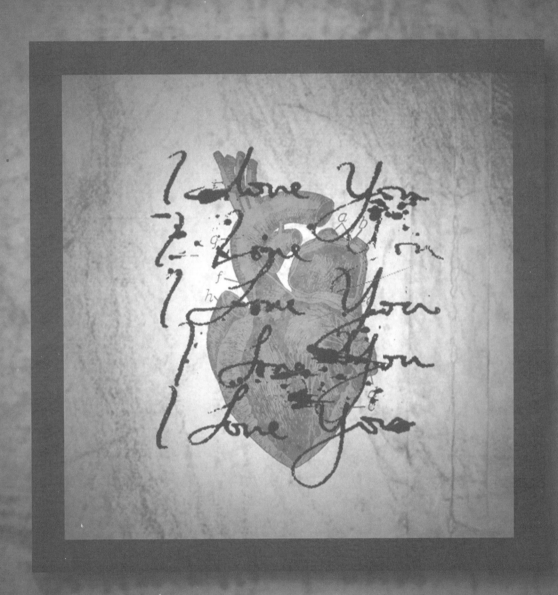

# I Love You

**Words and Music by Sarah McLachlan**

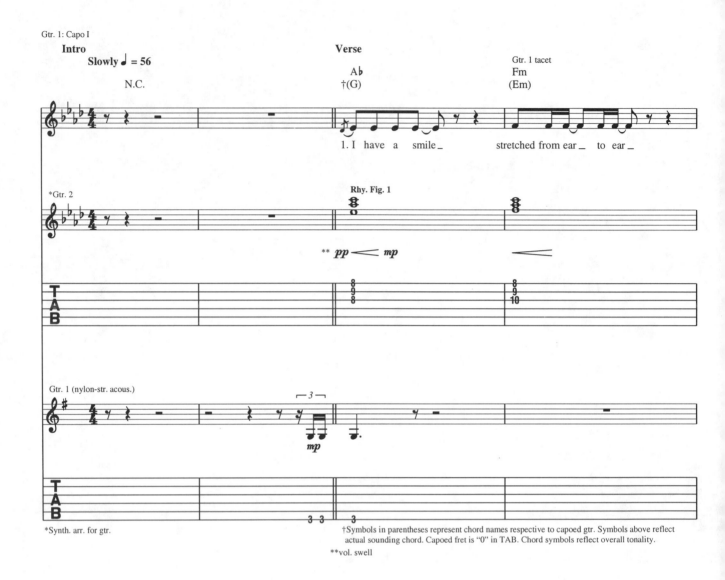

Gtr. 1: Capo I

**Intro**
**Slowly** ♩ = 56

**Verse**
Gtr. 1 tacet

*Synth. arr. for gtr.

†Symbols in parentheses represent chord names respective to capoed gtr. Symbols above reflect actual sounding chord. Capoed fret is "0" in TAB. Chord symbols reflect overall tonality.

**vol. swell

1. I have a smile _ stretched from ear _ to ear _

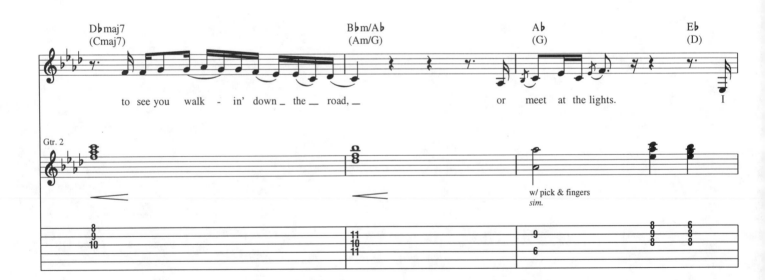

to see you walk - in' down _ the _ road, _ or meet at the lights. I

w/ pick & fingers
*sim.*

## Chorus

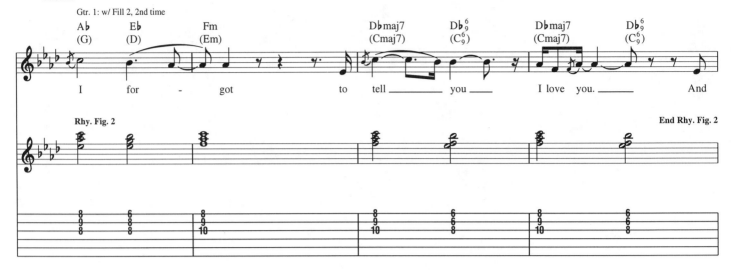

I for-got to tell \_\_\_\_\_ you \_\_\_\_\_ I love you. \_\_\_\_\_ And

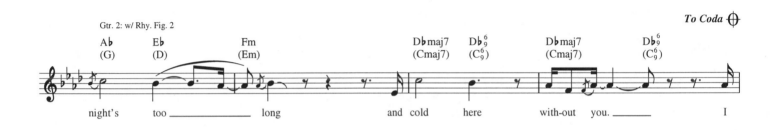

night's too \_\_\_\_\_ long and cold here with-out you. \_\_\_\_\_ I

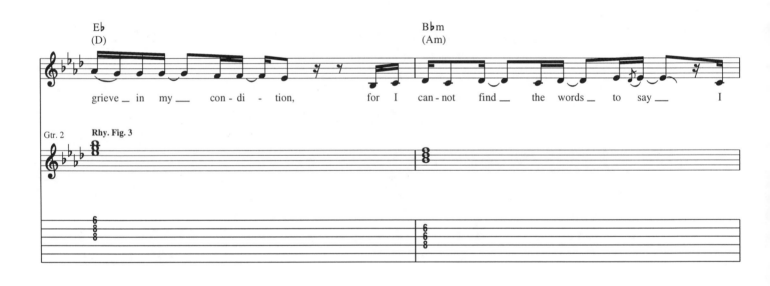

grieve \_\_ in my \_\_ con-di-tion, for I can-not find \_\_ the words \_\_ to say \_\_ I

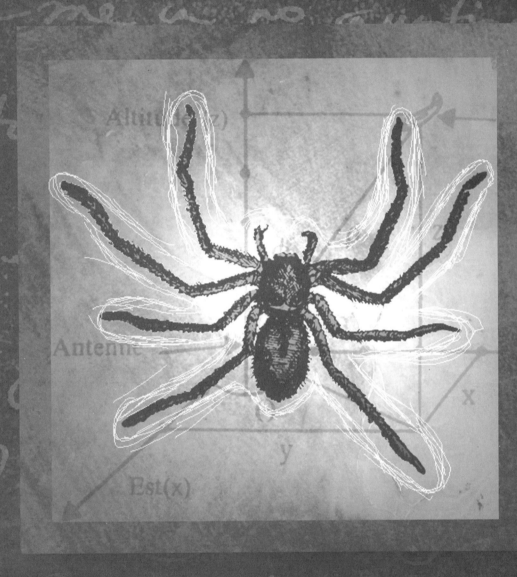

# Sweet Surrender

**Words and Music by Sarah McLachlan**

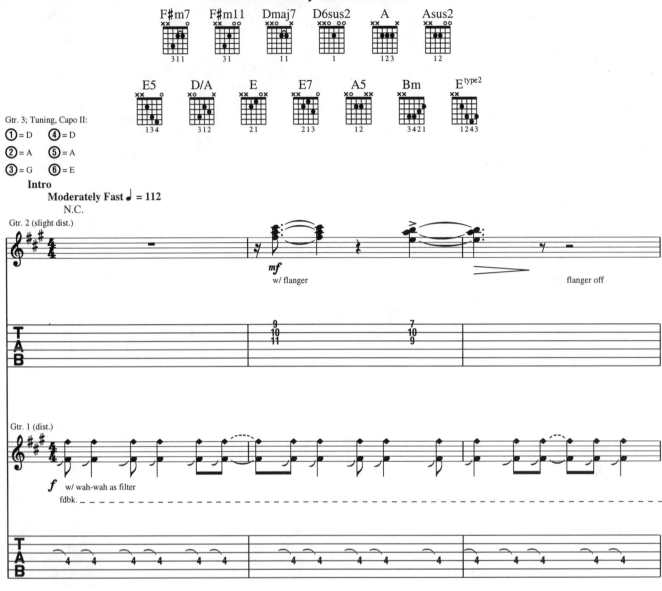

Gtr. 3; Tuning, Capo II:
① = D  ④ = D
② = A  ⑤ = A
③ = G  ⑥ = E

**Intro**
Moderately Fast ♩ = 112

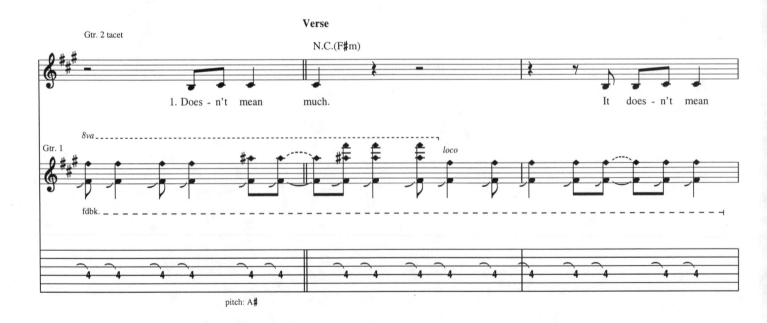

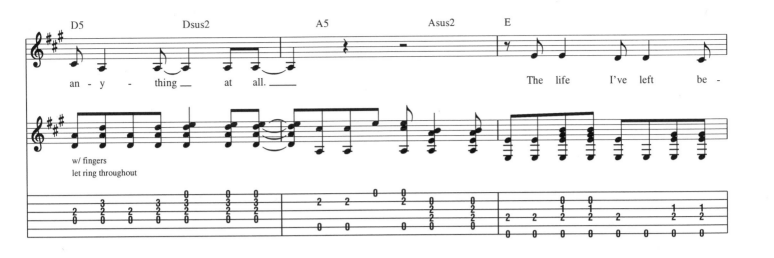

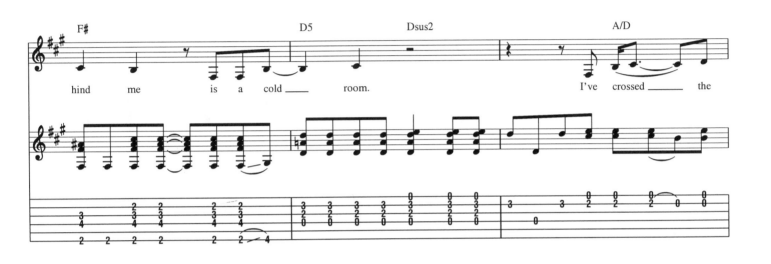

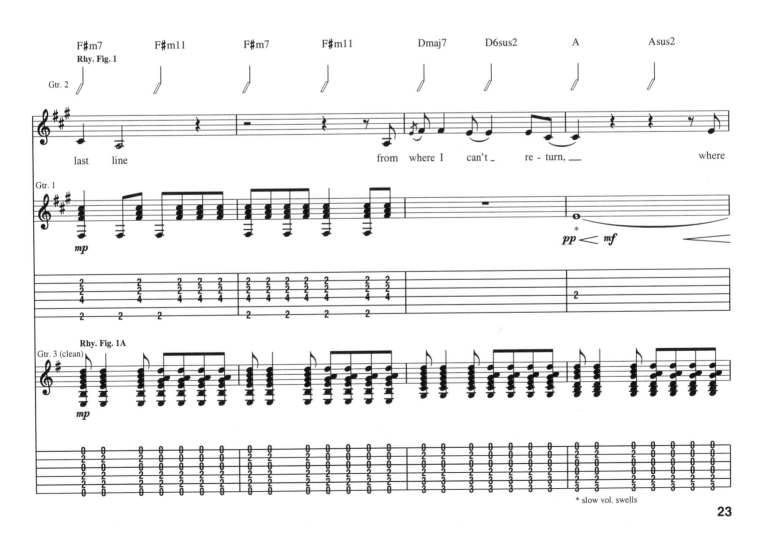

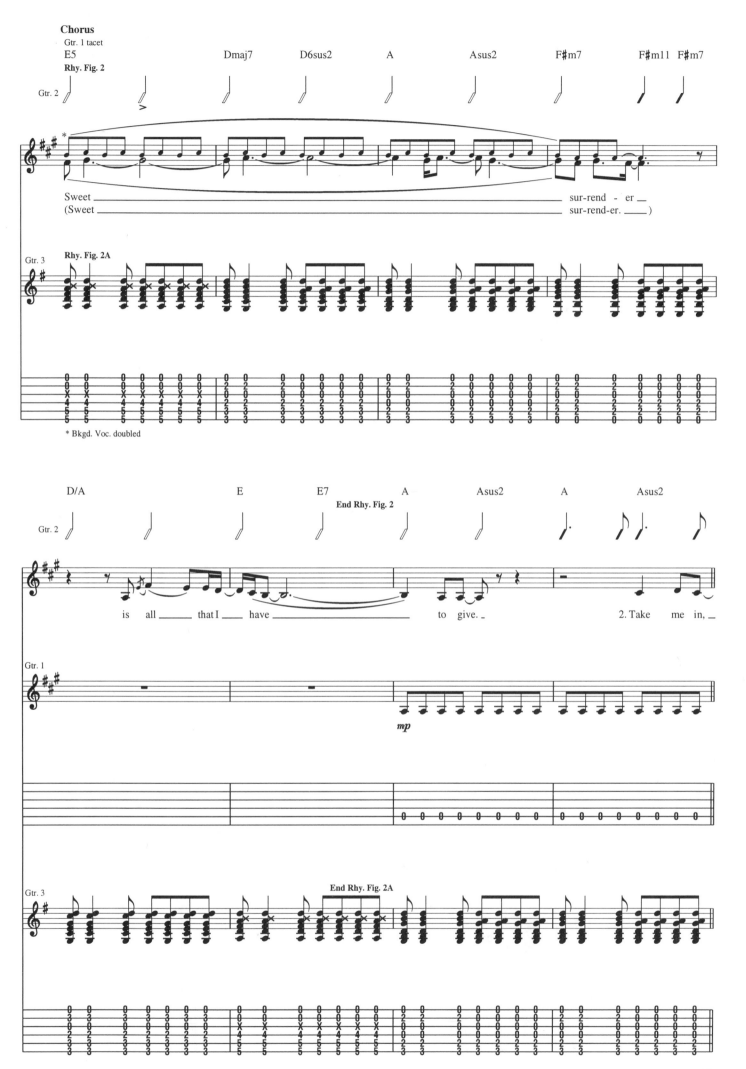

**Verse**

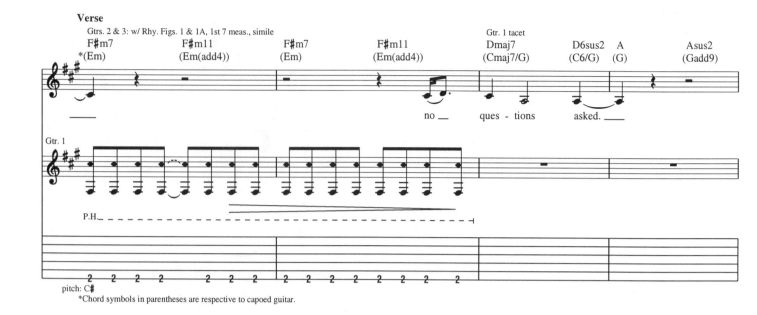

*Chord symbols in parentheses are respective to capoed guitar.

no __ ques - tions asked. __

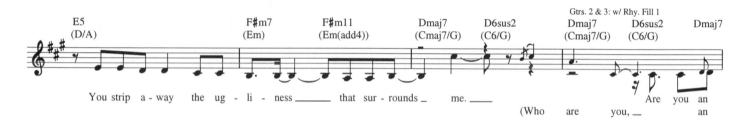

You strip a - way the ug - li - ness _____ that sur - rounds _ me. _____ (Who are you, __ an

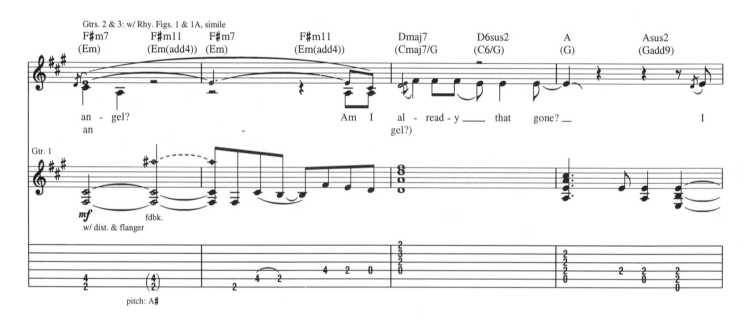

an - gel? Am I al - read - y ____ that gone? __ I
an - gel?)

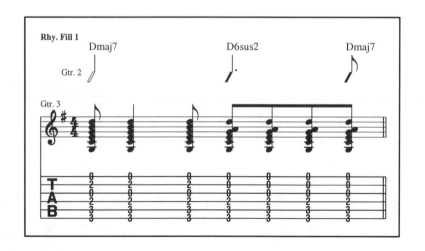

you all the beauty you p...

...only let yourself believ...

...at we are born innocent

...ou'd ...elieve

...at ...

me

it's easy we all falter

It's easy let it go...

It's easy let it go...

# Adia

**Words and Music by Sarah McLachlan and Pierre Marchand**

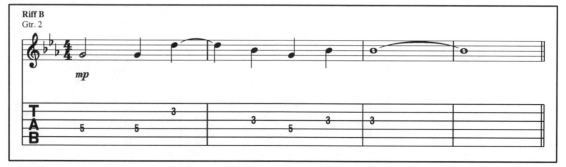

# Do What You Have to Do

### Words and Music by Sarah McLachlan and Colleen Wolstenholme

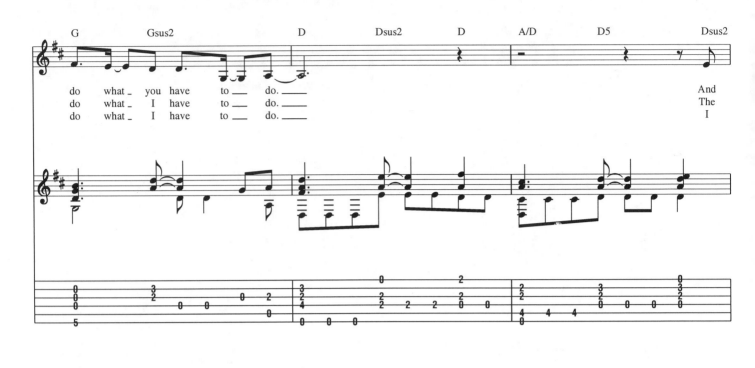

... (also called ... and ...
object lens) for the formation of an image of
the object under observation, and an *eyepiece* for
magnifying the image. These parts are set in

PRINCIPLE OF THE TELESCOPE
Explanation appears in text

a tube so constructed that the observer can
lengthen or shorten the distance between them.
Astronomical telescopes are of two types, re-
fracting and reflecting. In refractors the ob-

# Witness

**Words and Music by Sarah McLachlan and Pierre Marchand**

Gtrs. 2, 3, 4 & 6; Open E Tuning:
①= E  ④= E
②= B  ⑤= B
③= G#  ⑥= E

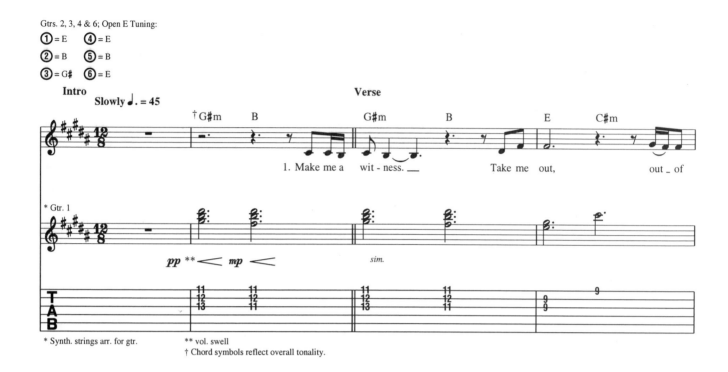

\* Synth. strings arr. for gtr.      \*\* vol. swell
† Chord symbols reflect overall tonality.

mis-er - y ___ made beau-ti - ful ___ right be - fore ___ our eyes? ___ Will

mer - cy ___ be re - vealed, __ or blind us ___ where we stand? Will we

**Chorus**

Gtrs. 2 & 3: w/ Rhy. Fig. 1, simile

burn ___ in ___ heav-en like we do ___ down

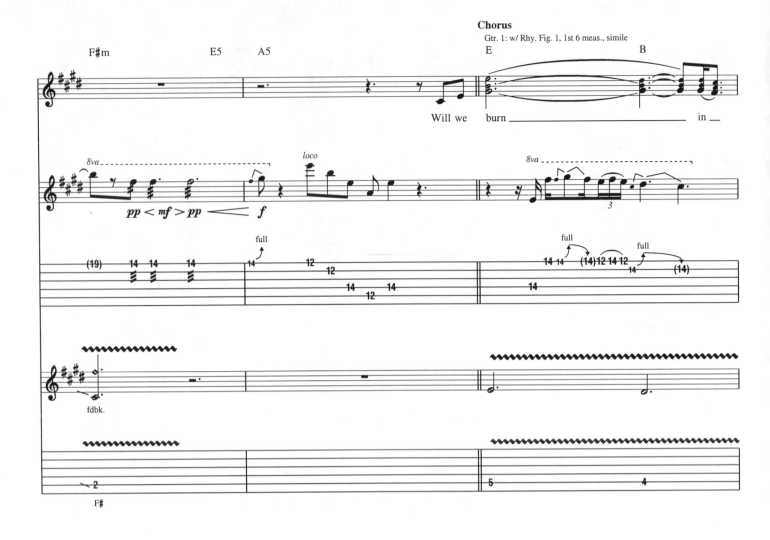

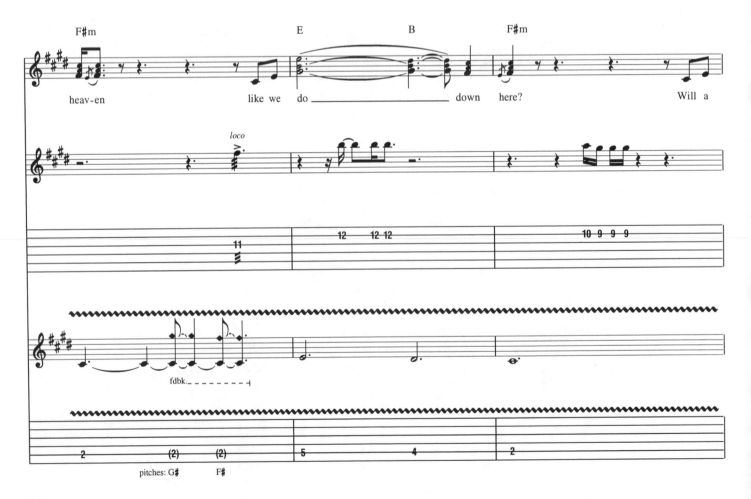

# Angel

**Words and Music by Sarah McLachlan**

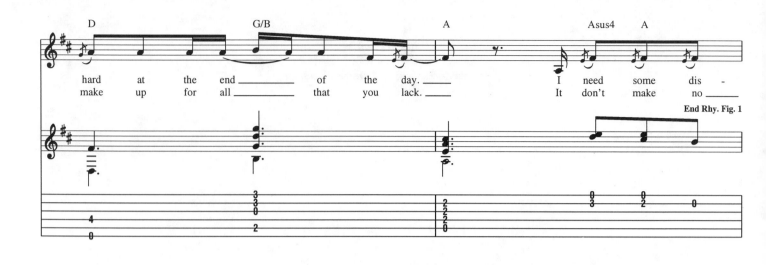

hard at the end _____ of the day. _____  I need some dis-
make up for all _____ that you lack. _____  It don't make no _____

**End Rhy. Fig. 1**

Gtr. 1: w/ Rhy. Fig. 1, simile

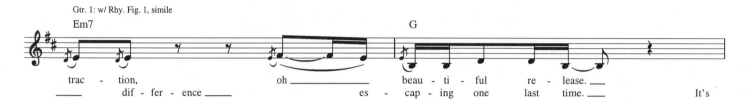

trac - tion,  oh _____  beau - ti - ful  re - lease. _____
_____ dif - fer - ence _____  es - cap - ing one last time. _____  It's

Mem - o - ry  seep  from my _____ veins.  Let me be
ea - si - er _____  to _____  be - lieve _____  in this sweet

emp - ty,  oh and  weight - less and  may - be  I'll find some peace to - night _____
mad - ness,  oh this  glo - ri - ous sad - ness  that brings me to _____ my

Gtr. 1

**Chorus**

knees. _____  In the { in the } arms of the an - gel.  Fly a - way _____ from here, _____

54

*To Coda* ⊕

**Coda**

**Outro**

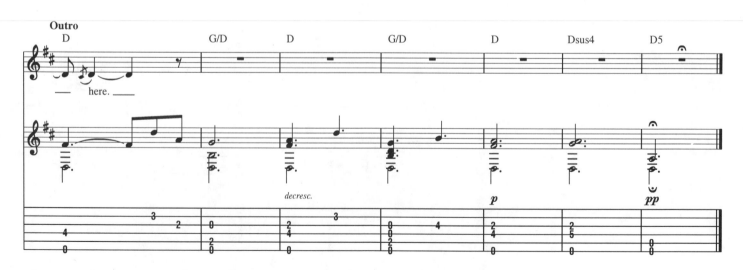

# Black & White

**Words and Music by Sarah McLachlan**

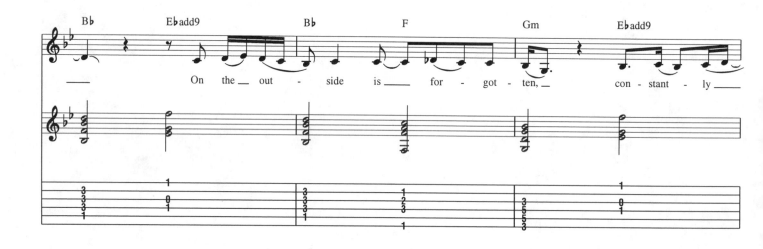

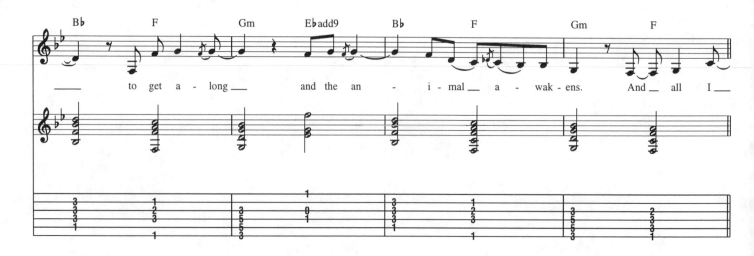

**Chorus**

Ev - 'ry - bod - y loves ___ you when ___ you're ea - sy. ___

Ev - 'ry - bod - y hates when you're ___ a bore. ___

Ev - 'ry - one ___ is wait - in' for ___ your en - trance, ___ so

w/ heavy reverb

don't ___ dis - ap - point ___ them. ___

\*Piano arr. for gtr.
\*\*Chord symbols reflect overall tonality.

†vol. swell

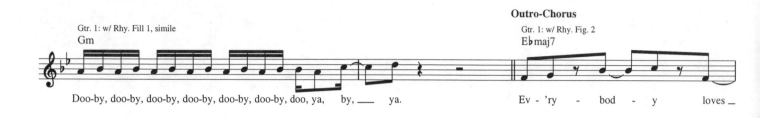

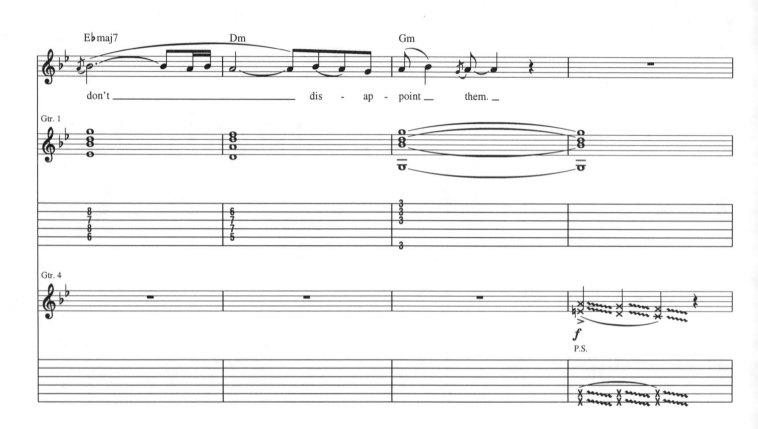

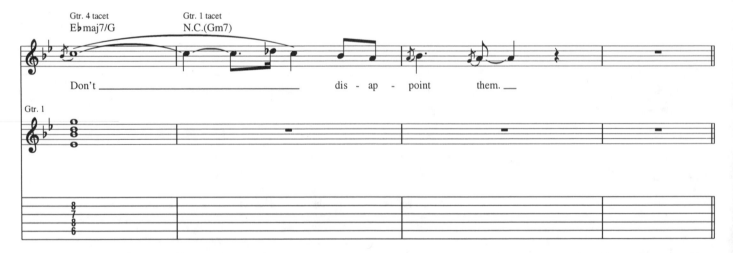

# Full of Grace

**Words and Music by Sarah McLachlan**

**Chorus**

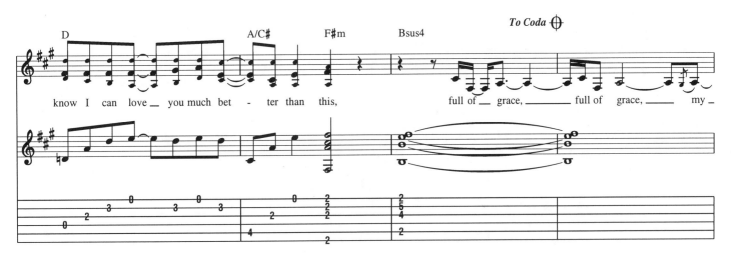

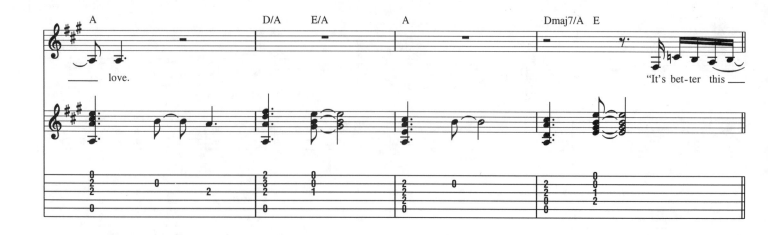

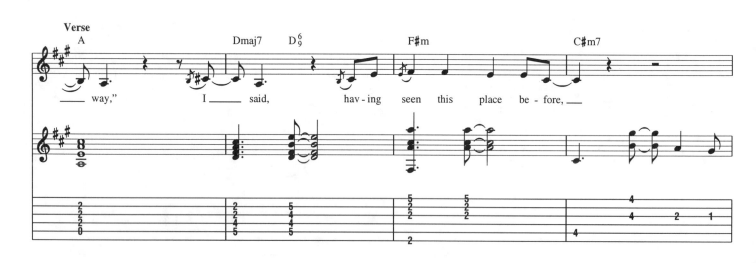

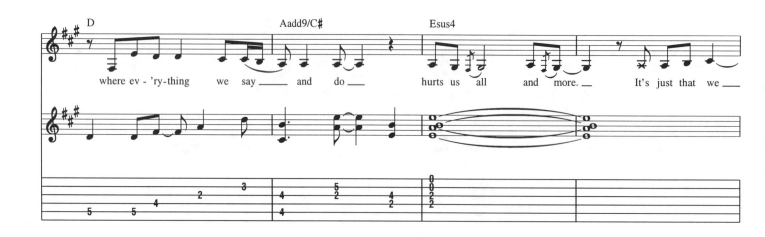

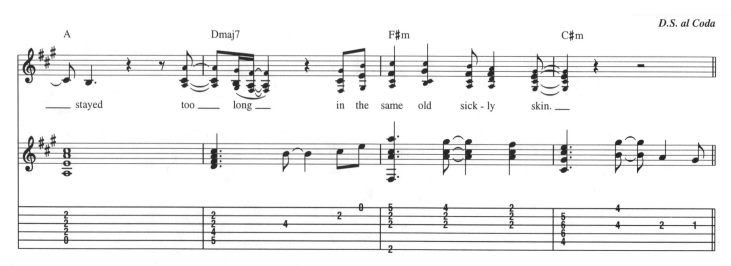

## Coda

**Outro**

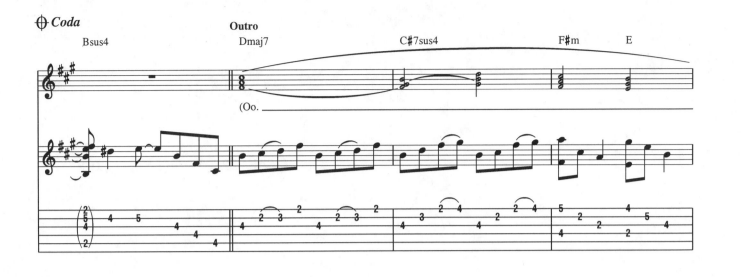

(Oo. _____

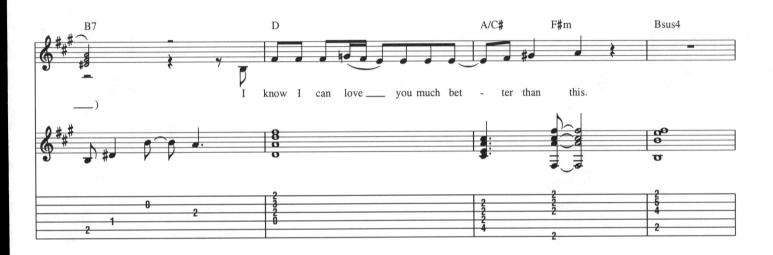

I know I can love ____ you much bet - ter than this.

____ )

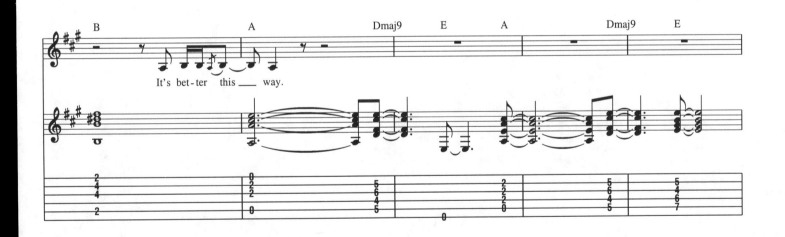

It's bet-ter this ____ way.

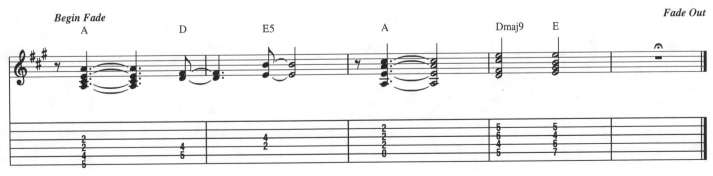

# Last Dance

**Words and Music by Sarah McLachlan**